MR. KURZEKA WAS ALL THE KID'S MOST FAVORITE NEIGHBOR. ALWAYS FUNNY AND SILLY, ESPECIALLY TOWARDS ME.

WE'D JOURNEY TO HIS HOUSE THROUGH THE ALLEY MOST DAYS TO CATCH A LAUGH, A SMILE, A CANDY TREAT — I WAS THREE.

HE WORKED HARD FOR THE CITY, AND HIS SNOWPLOW CLEANED MY STREET, BUT MY FAVORITE THING TO WATCH ON A WINTRY DAY WAS WHEN HE CLEARED THE HOCKEY SHEET.

WITH HIS BIG SPINNING BROOM, ACROSS THE ROAD I'D LOOK, HE'D WAVE TO ME THROUGH THE TRACTOR DOOR.
I'D SIT WISHING SOMEDAY I COULD JOIN HIM TO FEEL THE SOUND OF HIS ENGINE ROAR.

THEN ONE SNOWY MORNING, MY MOM WOKE ME UP WITH A SMILE AND SAID "MR. KURZEKA CALLED AND WAS WONDERING IF YOU WANTED TO RIDE IN HIS TRACTOR BED".

MY EXCITEMENT GREW AS I WALKED OUT THE DOOR. THE SNOW WAS UP TO MY CHIN.

HE MET ME HALF WAY WITH HIS ARMS EXTENDED. MY ADVENTURE WAS SOON TO BEGIN.

WE CLIMBED IN AND OFF WE WENT, HE SHOWED ME HOW TO BEEP THE HORN. 1 PASS, 2 PASS,

"BEEP, BEEP, BEEP"-

THEN DOWN THE MIDDLE WE SOARED.

SUDDENLY THEN I LOOKED AT HIM WONDERING WHY HE WAS TAKING A BOW –

HE LOOKED AT ME, HIS HANDS TO CHEST, SAYING "TOMMY, I'M GOING TO SLEEP NOW".

HE WENT TO SLEEP, JUST LIKE HE SAID, AS ONLY A THREE YEAR OLD COULD UNDERSTAND. BEEP, BEEP, BEEP, "WAKE UP, WAKE UP", BUT HE SLEPT EVEN WHEN WE HIT LAND.

THE BROOM KEPT SPINNING, ALTHOUGH WE WERE STILL. I CONTINUED MY WAKE-UP BEEPS. THE LOUD NOISE ECHOED THROUGHOUT THE BLOCK AND SOON PEOPLE CAME TO TAKE A PEEK.

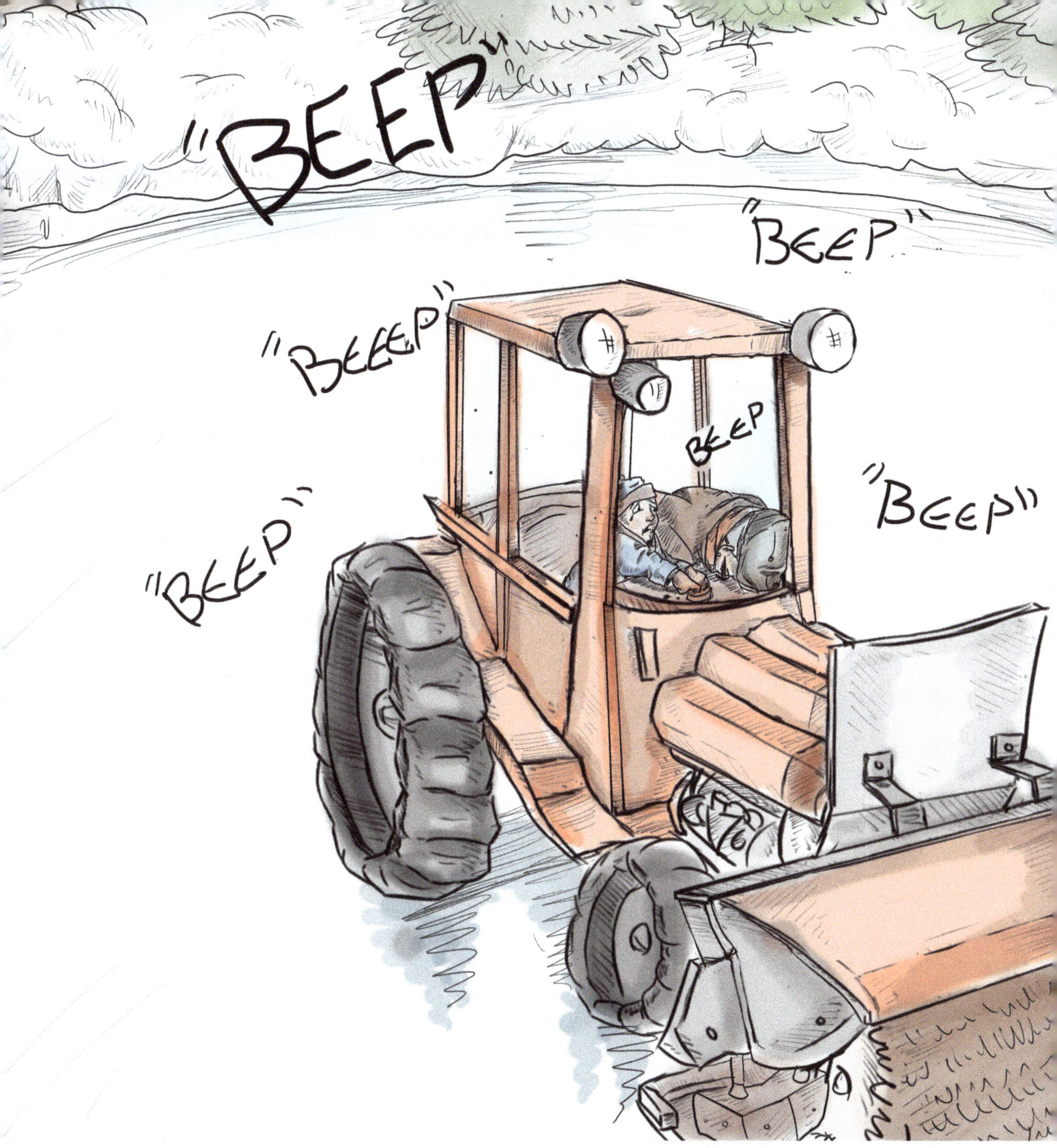
"BEEP"
"BEEP"
"BEEEP"
BEEP
"BEEP"
"BEEP"

MY JOY QUICKLY TURNED TO TEARS, MY MOM PULLED ME FROM THE TRACTOR. THE RIDE WAS OVER AND I WAS CONFUSED I HAD NO IDEA WHAT WAS THE MATTER.

OLDER NOW WITH YEARS
TO REFLECT
I WONDER ABOUT THIS
AND PRAY:
"WHY OF ALL PEOPLE, I
WAS CHOSEN TO BE WITH
HIM ON HIS LAST DAY?"

NO DIVINE EXPLANATION
HAS APPEARED TO ME
I'VE HAD TO SEARCH ON
MY OWN.
THE SEARCH HAS CAUSED
MY FAITH TO BLOSSOM
PERHAPS THAT WAS THE
REASON ALL ALONG.

HERE AND NOW, WHAT I DO KNOW, MR. KURZEKA WAS COURAGEOUS AND TRUE. WHO, DURING HIS LIFE'S MOST TOUGHEST MOMENT, GAVE COMFORT TO A KID WHO HE HARDLY KNEW.

He Turned Off the Rink Sweeper Before He Died

"I am going to sleep, Tommy..." The reassuring words did not disturb little three year old Tommy Porter as he joyfully rode in the cab of the snow broom, sweeping the Parkview Park rink Saturday morning of Friday's beautiful accumulation of snow. He was with his friend from the St. Louis Park Department of Parks.

Marven Kurzeka had carefully turned off the vehicle but the broom continued to revolve, attracting attention.

Tommy's older brother came running from their home across the street, as did his mother. Tommy was fine. His friend had suffered a massive heart attack.

Mr. Kurzeka, 50, of 3301 Louisiana Ave. had been with the Park Department eight years, after 25 years with the Milwaukee Road in their Bridge and Building Department.

He loved his work. He knew youngsters in every corner of St. Louis Park. He either was preparing playgounds or skating rinks. He coached football. He was a booster of basketball and other sports for kids.

He was an active member of Holy Family Catholic Church and the Men's Club, a familiar face at every fund raising event from Christmas tree sales to pancake breakfasts. He was a former treasurer of the Holy Family Home and School Association.

He was active in the St. Louis Council of the Knights of Columbus.

A veteran of World War II, he had been an Army Master Sergeant and had served overseas in Guam. He was a member of the VFW Post 5632 and the Frank Lundberg Post of the American Legion.

Survivors include his widow, Margaret; two sons, Richard and Lawrence; two daughters, Joanne and Louise; his sister, Mrs. George (Ruth) Mack, all of St. Louis Park; and two brothers, Raymond of Hidden Hills, Calif. and William of Canoga Park, Calif.

Requiem Mass was offered yesterday at Holy Family Church. Burial was in Fort Snelling National Cemetery.

St. Louis Park, MN – Park & Recreation Staff (circ. Early 1960's)

Dick Bren, Herman Freiborg, George Haun, Dick Gatzmer, Fran Callahan, Pauline Cheleen, Bill Reiners, Tony Mackert, Marv Kurzeka, LeRoy Thies, Jerry Woodbury

"He Turned Off the Rink Sweeper Before he Died", St. Louis Park Dispatch - Vol. 35, No. 33. Dateline: Thursday, January 19, 1967.

www.ingramcontent.com/pod-product-compliance
Lightning Source LLC
Chambersburg PA
CBHW061818290426
44110CB00026B/2909